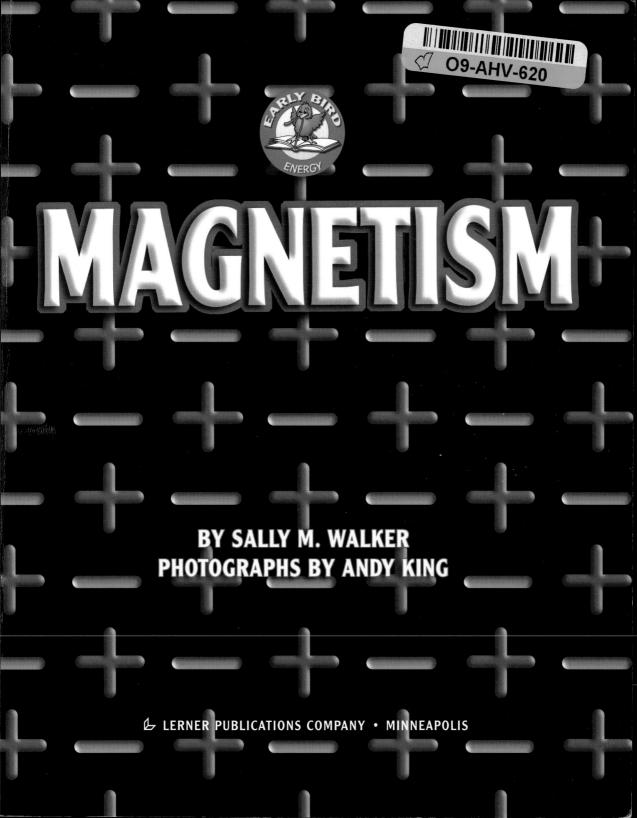

EARLY BIRD
ENERGY

MAGNETISM

BY SALLY M. WALKER
PHOTOGRAPHS BY ANDY KING

LERNER PUBLICATIONS COMPANY · MINNEAPOLIS

O9-AHV-620

Additional photographs are reproduced with permission from: PhotoDisc Royalty Free by Getty Images, p. 8; © Arthur R. Hill/Visuals Unlimited, p. 12; © Owaki-Kulla/CORBIS, p. 40; © Gerry Lemmo, p. 42.

Text copyright © 2006 by Sally M. Walker
Photographs copyright © 2006 by Andy King, except as noted

All rights reserved. International copyright secured. No part of this book may be reproduced, stored in a retrieval system, or transmitted in any form or by any means—electronic, mechanical, photocopying, recording, or otherwise—without the prior written permission of Lerner Publishing Group, except for the inclusion of brief quotations in an acknowledged review.

Lerner Publications Company
A division of Lerner Publishing Group
241 First Avenue North
Minneapolis, MN 55401 U.S.A.

Website address: www.lernerbooks.com

Library of Congress Cataloging-in-Publication Data

Walker, Sally M.
    Magnetism / by Sally M. Walker.
        p.   cm. — (Early bird energy)
    Includes index.
    ISBN-13: 978–0–8225–2932–3 (lib. bdg. : alk. paper)
    ISBN-10: 0–8225–2932–7 (lib. bdg. : alk. paper)
    1. Magnetism—Juvenile literature. 2. Magnetism—Experiments—Juvenile literature.
3. Magnets—Juvenile literature. I. Title. II. Series: Walker, Sally M. Early bird energy.
    QC753.7.W35 2006
    538—dc22   2005009037

Manufactured in the United States of America
1 2 3 4 5 6 – BP – 11 10 09 08 07 06

CONTENTS

BE A WORD DETECTIVE

Can you find these words as you read about magnetism?
Be a detective and try to figure out what they mean.
You can turn to the glossary on page 46 for help.

atoms	magnetic	permanent
compass	magnetic field	poles
electromagnets	nonmagnetic	repel
electrons	nucleus	temporary
force	orbit	unlike

Some magnets are easy to see. Other magnets are hidden inside machines. What do the hidden magnets do?

CHAPTER 1
MAGNETS

Look around your home or classroom. Do you see any magnets? Many people use magnets to hold pictures on their refrigerators. These magnets are easy to see.

There are also many magnets that you can't see. They are hidden inside radios, telephones, and TV sets. Why are magnets inside these machines?

A magnet makes magnetic force. A force is a push or pull. Magnetic force makes a magnet stick to a refrigerator. Forces from hidden magnets make many machines work.

Without magnets, TV sets wouldn't work.

A magnet's force begins with tiny particles called atoms. Everything is made of atoms. Magnets, air, plants, rocks, and your body are made of atoms. Billions of atoms could fit on the dot above the letter *i*. The center of an atom is called the nucleus (NOO-klee-uhs).

Everything around you is made of atoms. You are made of atoms too!

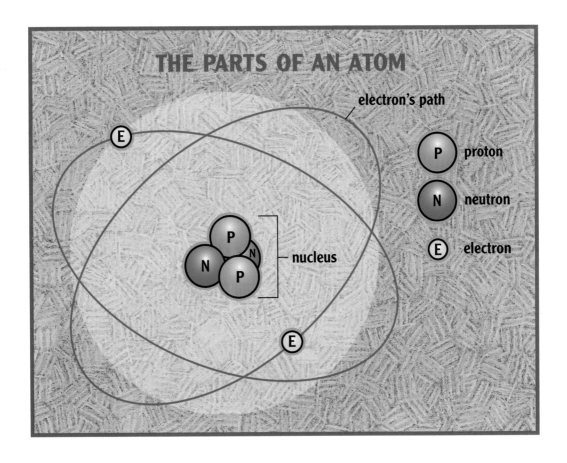

THE PARTS OF AN ATOM

electron's path

E

P proton

N neutron

E electron

P
N
N
P

nucleus

E

Atoms are made of even smaller particles. These particles are called protons, neutrons (NOO-trahnz), and electrons. An atom's nucleus is made of protons and neutrons. Electrons orbit around an atom's nucleus. Orbiting is traveling in a circle. A little bit of a magnet's force is made by electrons orbiting inside it.

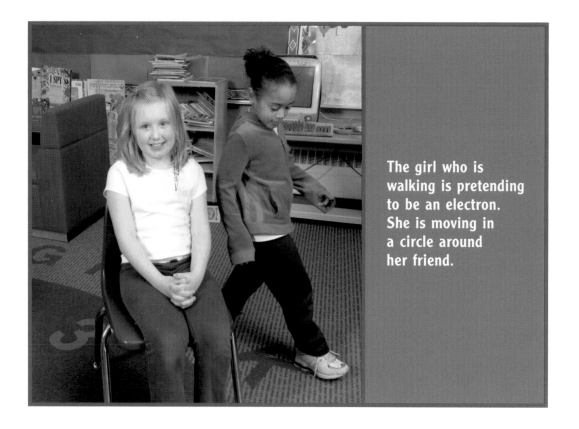

The girl who is walking is pretending to be an electron. She is moving in a circle around her friend.

Ask a friend to sit in the middle of the room. Walk in a circle around your friend. You are orbiting your friend.

While an electron is orbiting, it also moves in a second way. Stop walking and stand in place. Spin your body around. An electron spins this way too. Most of a magnet's force comes from electrons spinning inside it.

An atom's electrons spin in different directions. Some electrons spin clockwise. The rest spin counterclockwise. Sometimes half of an atom's electrons spin clockwise and half spin counterclockwise. Then the atom has no magnetic force. But if more electrons spin one way than the other, the atom has magnetic force. Atoms that have magnetic force act like tiny magnets.

Now the girl is spinning in place. An electron spins while it is moving in a circle around a nucleus.

Strong magnets lift heavy pieces of metal in junkyards. Do all magnets keep their magnetic force forever?

CHAPTER 2

MAGNETIC MATERIALS

Some magnets are stronger than others. Strong magnets have more magnetic force than weak magnets. Bar magnets, horseshoe magnets, and round magnets are strong. But rubbery refrigerator magnets are weak.

Some magnets are permanent magnets. Permanent magnets keep their magnetic force forever. Other magnets are temporary magnets.

Temporary magnets keep their magnetic force for a while. But then it goes away.

A kind of black rock called lodestone is a permanent magnet. Some metals can become permanent magnets too. Iron, nickel, steel, and cobalt are metals that can be made into permanent magnets. Materials that can be made into magnets are called magnetic materials.

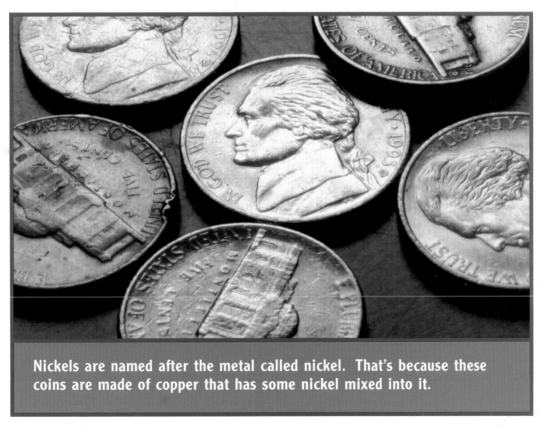

Nickels are named after the metal called nickel. That's because these coins are made of copper that has some nickel mixed into it.

A magnet attracts other magnetic materials. The magnet's force pulls on the magnetic material. The pulling force makes the magnetic material stick to the magnet. Magnets stick to any magnetic material.

A magnet sticks to any magnetic material.

Paper clips are made of steel. Magnets attract objects that are made of steel.

Get a magnet and a paper clip. Can you pick up the paper clip with the magnet? Yes. The magnet attracts the paper clip. The paper clip is made of steel. Steel is a magnetic material.

Most materials are nonmagnetic. Magnets don't attract nonmagnetic materials. And nonmagnetic materials can't be made into magnets. The metals aluminum, copper, and silver are nonmagnetic. So are rubber, wood, and concrete.

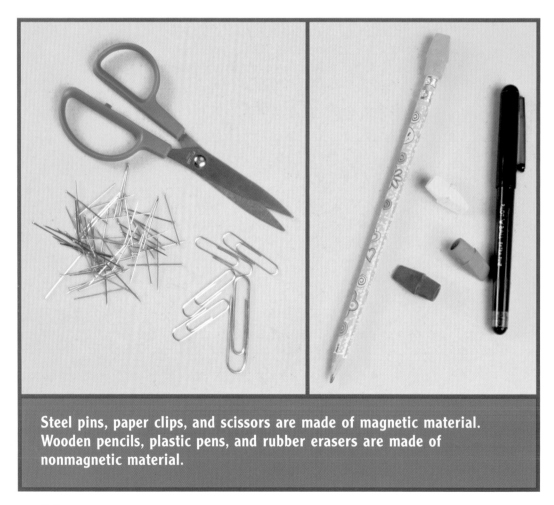

Steel pins, paper clips, and scissors are made of magnetic material. Wooden pencils, plastic pens, and rubber erasers are made of nonmagnetic material.

A magnet can't pick up a wooden pencil.

Use your magnet to find out if materials are magnetic. Does your magnet stick to the glass in a window? Can your magnet pick up a pencil? Test other materials. See if they are magnetic or not.

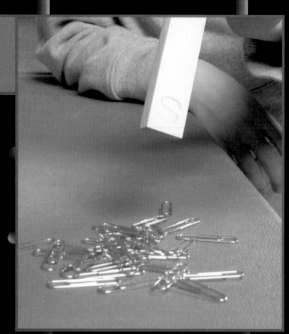

Magnets attract steel objects like paper clips. Why isn't this magnet attracting the paper clips?

CHAPTER 3
HOW MAGNETS WORK

Every magnet has a magnetic field. The magnetic field is a space around the magnet. Inside this space, the magnet's force can attract an object. If magnetic material is outside the field, the magnet can't attract it. You can prove this. You'll need a magnet, a metal paper clip, and a piece of thread.

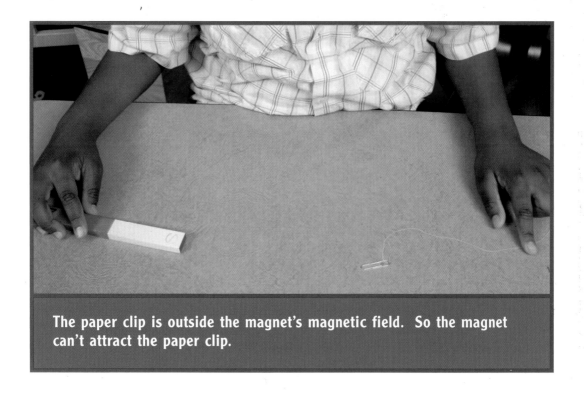

The paper clip is outside the magnet's magnetic field. So the magnet can't attract the paper clip.

Tie one end of the thread to the paper clip. Put the paper clip on a table. Use your finger to hold the thread's loose end against the table. Put the magnet about 10 inches away from the paper clip. Move the magnet up and down. Is the paper clip attracted to the magnet? No. The paper clip just stays still. The paper clip is outside the magnetic field. The magnet can't attract the paper clip.

Put the magnet about half an inch from the paper clip. Lift the magnet up and down. What happens now? The paper clip moves. It is inside the magnetic field.

The paper clip is inside the magnet's magnetic field. The magnet makes the paper clip move.

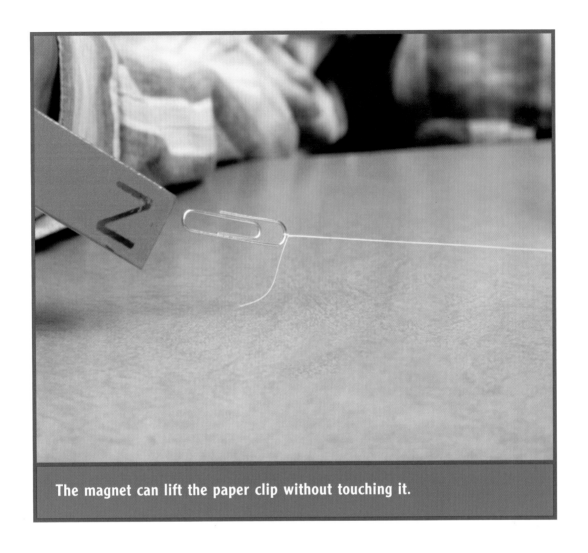

The magnet can lift the paper clip without touching it.

Magnetic force is strongest close to the magnet. Sometimes the force is strong enough to lift an object without touching it. Can your magnet lift the paper clip off the table without touching it?

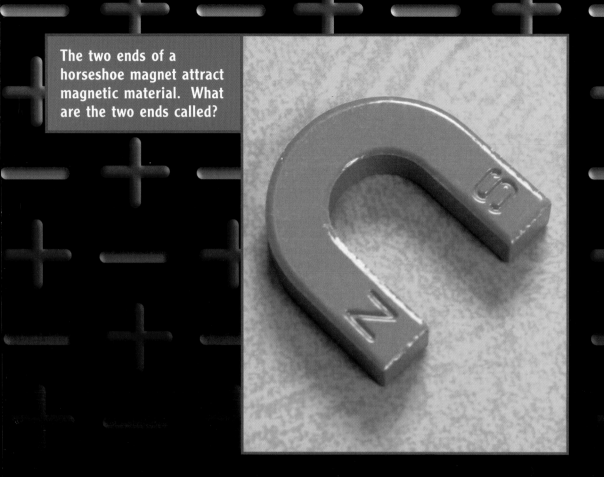

The two ends of a horseshoe magnet attract magnetic material. What are the two ends called?

CHAPTER 4
MAGNETIC POLES

Two parts of a magnet have the strongest
pulling power. These parts are called poles.
Every magnet has two poles. One is called the
north pole. The other is called the south pole.

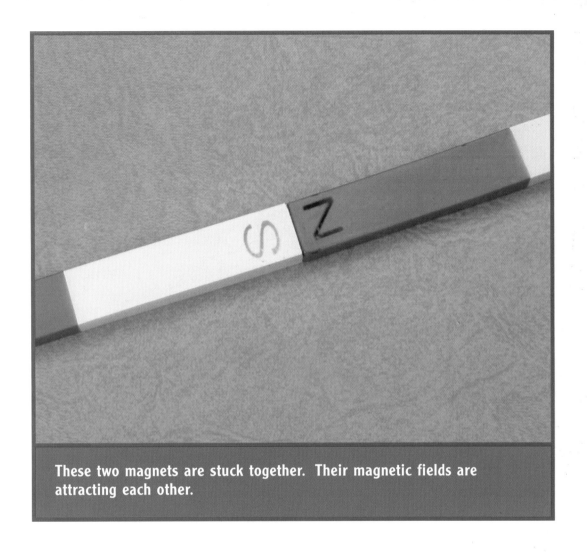

These two magnets are stuck together. Their magnetic fields are attracting each other.

The magnetic field of one magnet can affect the magnetic field of another magnet. The two magnetic fields push or pull at each other. The magnets try to line up so both magnetic fields point in the same direction.

Earth has a magnetic field. So Earth has a magnetic north pole. If you hang a magnet from a string, it turns so its magnetic field lines up with Earth's field. The magnet's north pole will always point toward Earth's magnetic north pole. The needle of a compass is a magnet. The needle's north pole turns until it points toward Earth's magnetic north pole.

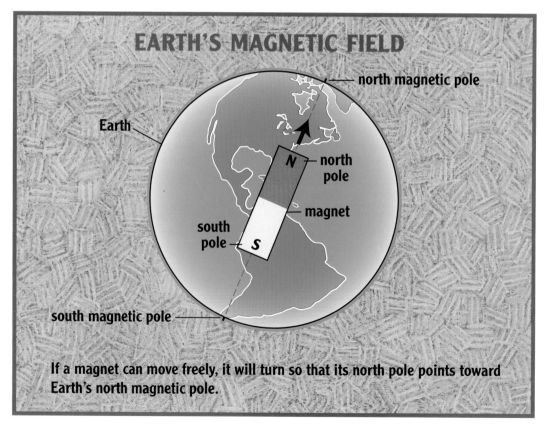

EARTH'S MAGNETIC FIELD

north magnetic pole

Earth

north pole

magnet

south pole

south magnetic pole

If a magnet can move freely, it will turn so that its north pole points toward Earth's north magnetic pole.

For this experiment, the bowl must be wider than the length of the magnets.

You can find a magnet's north pole. You will need two small bar magnets, a thick foam tray, scissors, tape, a pen, a compass, and a large bowl of water.

Cut two strips of foam. Each strip should be longer and wider than the magnets. Tape one magnet to each foam strip. Draw an *X* on the foam next to one end of each magnet. The *X* will help you tell the ends apart.

If the foam is too thin, the magnet will not float. If your magnet doesn't float, cut extra strips of foam. Tape three or four strips together to make one thick strip of foam.

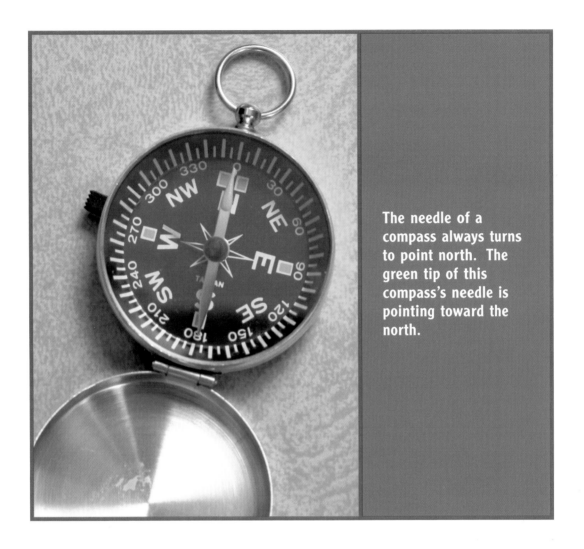

The needle of a compass always turns to point north. The green tip of this compass's needle is pointing toward the north.

Put the compass about 1 foot away from the bowl of water. The needle of the compass will turn. Wait for it to stop moving. Notice which direction it is pointing. That direction is north.

Float one of the magnets in the bowl of water. Watch as the magnet turns. One end always turns toward the north. That end is the magnet's north pole. The other end is the south pole. Turn the float around, then let go. The magnet will turn back around to point north.

Put a tiny piece of tape on the magnet's north pole. Mark it with an *N*. Find the other magnet's north pole the same way.

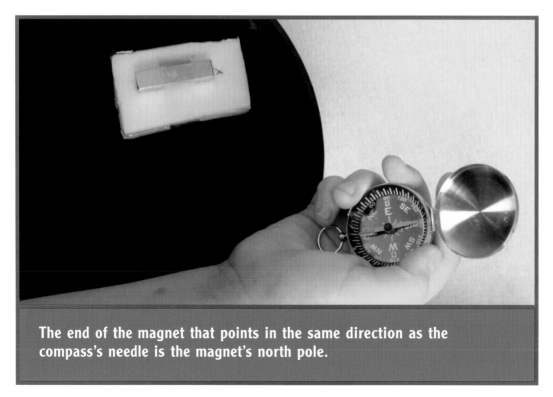

The end of the magnet that points in the same direction as the compass's needle is the magnet's north pole.

Even if you push hard, you can't make two north poles touch.

Take the magnets off the foam floats. Hold each magnet by its south pole. Try to make the two north poles touch. What happens? The magnets push away from each other. Hold the two north poles. Try to touch the south poles together. The same thing happens. Why? Because poles that are alike repel (ree-PEHL) each other. Repelling is pushing away.

Hold one magnet by its north pole. Hold the other magnet by its south pole. Now try to touch the magnets together. What happens? They stick together. Why? Because unlike poles attract each other. Unlike poles are poles that are different.

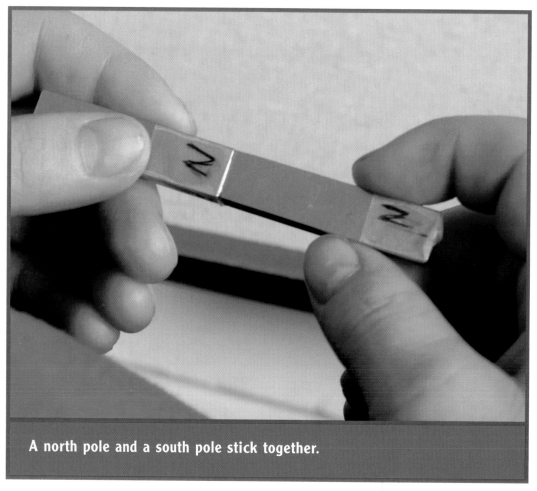

A north pole and a south pole stick together.

Use the north pole of one magnet to push against the north pole of the other magnet.

Put one magnet on a table. Can you push the magnet off the table without touching it? Push it with magnetic force. Remember that like poles repel each other. And unlike poles attract each other.

Magnetic force can work through nonmagnetic materials. Cover a paper clip with a piece of paper. Hold a magnet very close to the paper. Lift the magnet. What happens? The magnetic force passes through the paper. The magnet attracts the paper clip. The magnet lifts both the paper and the paper clip.

The magnet's force works through a piece of paper.

A strong magnet's force even works through your finger!

Magnetic force can act through your body too. Use your right hand to hold a magnet on top of your left pointer finger. Ask a friend to hold a paper clip under your finger, just below the magnet. Can your friend make the paper clip hang from your finger?

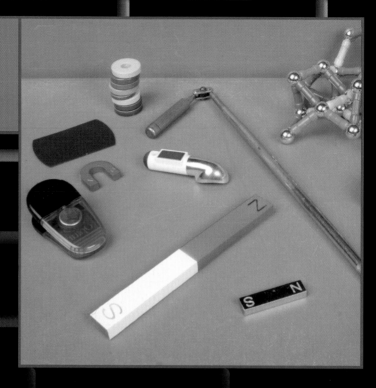

All magnets are made of materials that have magnetic force. Why do these materials have magnetic force?

CHAPTER 5
KINDS OF MAGNETS

Some materials have many atoms with magnetic force. These atoms line up so their poles all point in the same direction. Because the magnetic atoms are lined up this way, the material has a lot of magnetic force.

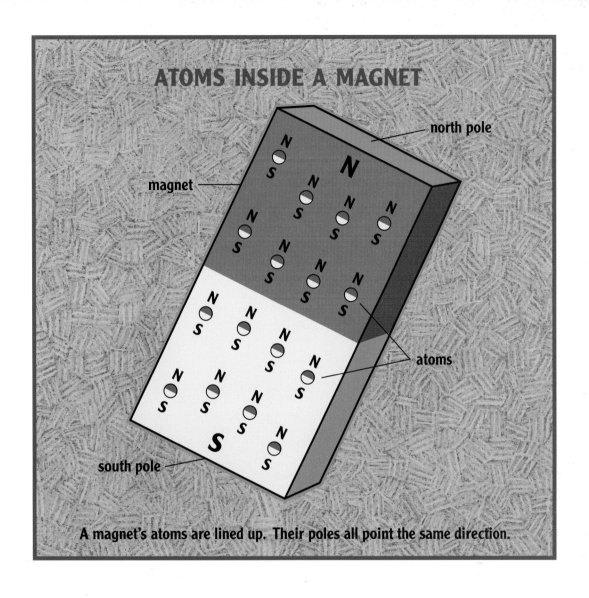

ATOMS INSIDE A MAGNET

north pole

magnet

atoms

south pole

A magnet's atoms are lined up. Their poles all point the same direction.

Iron and steel have many atoms with magnetic force. So objects made of iron and steel can become temporary magnets. You can prove this with two paper clips and a magnet.

Hold one paper clip near the other paper clip. Try to pick up the other clip with the first one. Are the paper clips attracted to each other? No. There is no magnetic force between them.

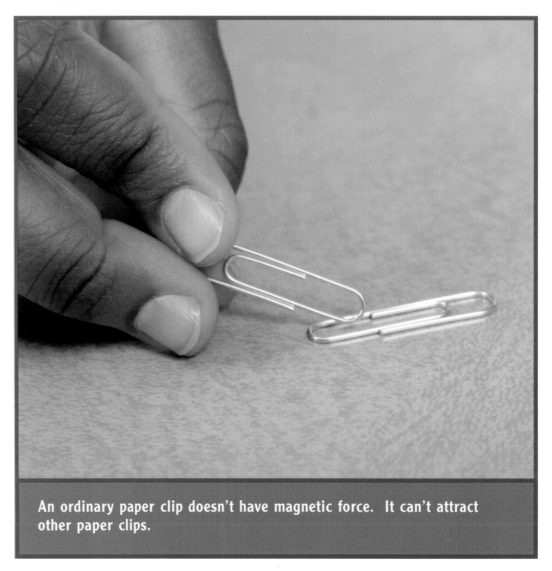

An ordinary paper clip doesn't have magnetic force. It can't attract other paper clips.

Sticking a paper clip onto a magnet gives the clip magnetic force. Then the clip can attract another paper clip.

Put one paper clip onto the magnet. Make sure one end of the clip sticks out. Hold the magnet so that the loose end of the clip is near the other paper clip. Is it attracted to the hanging paper clip? It is. Why does this happen?

A paper clip's atoms are like tiny magnets. The magnet's force makes the atoms line up so their poles point in the same direction. The paper clip becomes a temporary magnet.

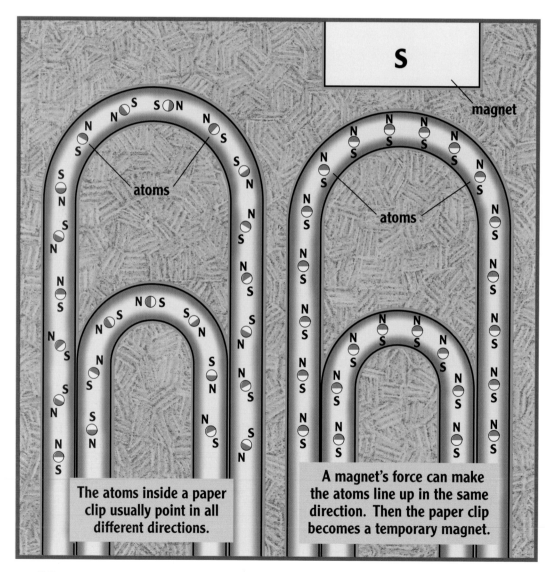

The atoms inside a paper clip usually point in all different directions.

A magnet's force can make the atoms line up in the same direction. Then the paper clip becomes a temporary magnet.

Tapping the paper clip on the table takes away the clip's magnetic force.

Sharply tap your paper clip magnet against a tabletop 50 times. Then hold it near the other paper clips. Does it attract them now? No. Tapping the paper clip knocked the atoms out of their neat lines. The magnetic force is gone.

Electricity can be used to make very strong temporary magnets. These magnets are called electromagnets. To make an electromagnet, wire is twisted into a coil. The wire can carry electricity. When electricity flows through the coil of wire, it makes a strong magnetic field. When the electricity is turned off, the magnetic force stops.

Most doorbells have an electromagnet inside them. The electromagnet makes the bell ring.

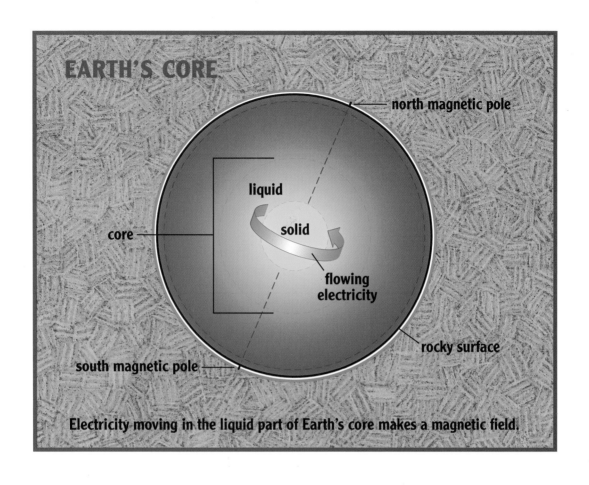

EARTH'S CORE

north magnetic pole

liquid

solid

core

flowing electricity

rocky surface

south magnetic pole

Electricity moving in the liquid part of Earth's core makes a magnetic field.

The center of Earth is called the core. Earth's core is mostly made of iron. The core is very hot. So some of the iron in the core is melted. This melted iron is not a hard metal. Instead, it is a liquid. Electricity moves around in the liquid iron. The flowing electricity makes a magnetic field. Earth is a giant electromagnet!

Some animals can sense Earth's magnetic field. Birds use Earth's magnetic field to find their way when they migrate. Migrating is traveling when the seasons change.

Some geese travel thousands of miles each year. The geese may use Earth's magnetic field to find their way.

Magnets make the letters and pictures you see on a computer screen.

Magnetic force is an important part of our lives. Magnets are inside most of the machines we use. Tiny magnets are inside computers. Large magnets lift heavy objects in junkyards. Magnets make our work easier. What magnets are working for you right now?

A NOTE TO ADULTS
ON SHARING A BOOK

When you share a book with a child, you show that reading is important. To get the most out of the experience, read in a comfortable, quiet place. Turn off the television and limit other distractions, such as telephone calls. Be prepared to start slowly. Take turns reading parts of this book. Stop occasionally and discuss what you're reading. Talk about the photographs. If the child begins to lose interest, stop reading. When you pick up the book again, revisit the parts you have already read.

BE A VOCABULARY DETECTIVE

The word list on page 5 contains words that are important in understanding the topic of this book. Be word detectives and search for the words as you read the book together. Talk about what the words mean and how they are used in the sentence. Do any of these words have more than one meaning? You will find the words defined in a glossary on page 46.

WHAT ABOUT QUESTIONS?

Use questions to make sure the child understands the information in this book. Here are some suggestions:

> What did this paragraph tell us? What does this picture show? How do people use magnets? What are the two ways that an electron moves? Which parts of a magnet have the strongest pulling power? How does a compass show direction? What is your favorite part of the book? Why?

If the child has questions, don't hesitate to respond with questions of your own, such as: What do *you* think? Why? What is it that you don't know? If the child can't remember certain facts, turn to the index.

INTRODUCING THE INDEX

The index helps readers find information without searching through the whole book. Turn to the index on page 48. Choose an entry such as *magnetic poles* and ask the child to use the index to find out which poles repel each other. Repeat with as many entries as you like. Ask the child to point out the differences between an index and a glossary. (The index helps readers find information, while the glossary tells readers what words mean.)

LEARN MORE ABOUT MAGNETISM

BOOKS

Farndon, John. *Magnetism*. Tarrytown, NY: Benchmark Books, 2002. Find out all about magnetism, including many ways that people use magnets.

Gibson, Gary. *Playing with Magnets*. Brookfield, CT: Copper Beech Books, 1995. Try these games and activities to learn more about magnetism.

Meiani, Antonella. *Magnetism*. Minneapolis: Lerner Publications Company, 2003. Simple experiments show how magnets work.

Nankivell-Aston, Sally, and Dorothy Jackson. *Science Experiments with Magnets*. New York: Franklin Watts, 2000. This book is packed with experiments and activities using magnets.

Tocci, Salvatore. *Experiments with Magnets*. New York: Children's Press, 2001. This book has more experiments to help you learn about magnets.

WEBSITES

Compass Points
http://www.nationalgeographic.com/ngkids/trythis/tryfun2.html
Find out how to make a compass.

Creative Kids at Home: Magnets
http://www.creativekidsathome.com/science/magnet.html
This website has trivia questions, activities, and more.

Energy Kids Page: Energy History
http://www.eia.doe.gov/kids/history/index.html
Learn about the history of energy, including magnetism. This website also has information about some of the famous scientists who figured out how energy works.

GLOSSARY

atoms: the particles that make up all things

compass: a tool used to show direction. A compass's needle is a magnet that always points north.

electromagnets: magnets that get their magnetic force from electricity

electrons: tiny particles that circle around the center of an atom

force: a push or pull

magnetic: can be made into a magnet. Iron and steel are magnetic materials.

magnetic field: the space around a magnet where the magnet's force can attract an object

nonmagnetic: cannot be made into a magnet. Paper and glass are nonmagnetic materials.

nucleus (NOO-klee-uhs): the center of an atom

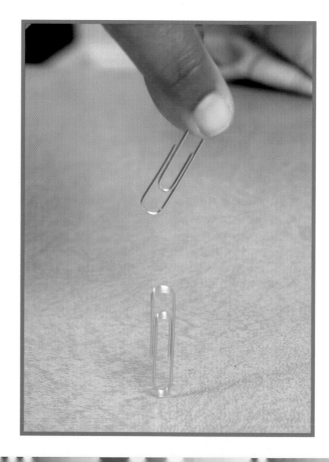

orbit: to travel in a circle

permanent: lasting forever

poles: the two parts of a magnet that have the strongest pulling power. Every magnet has a north pole and a south pole.

repel (ree-PEHL): to push away

temporary: lasting only for a short time

unlike: different

INDEX

Pages listed in **bold** type refer to photographs.

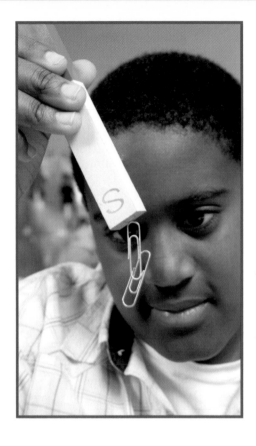